WE WANT JOBS!

A Story of the Great Depression

by **Robert J. Norrell**

Alex Haley, General Editor

Illustrations by Jan Naimo Jones

STECK-VAUGHN
COMPANY
A Subsidiary of National Education Corporation

For Katie

Published by Steck-Vaughn Company.
Text, illustrations, and cover art copyright © 1993 by Dialogue
Systems, Inc., 627 Broadway, New York, New York 10012.
All rights reserved.

Cover art by Jan Naimo Jones

Printed in the United States of America
1 2 3 4 5 6 7 8 9 R 98 97 96 95 94 93 92

Library of Congress Cataloging-in-Publication Data

Norrell, Robert J. (Robert Jefferson)
    We want jobs!: a story of the Great Depression/author, Robert
J. Norrell; illustrator, Jan Naimo Jones.
        p.   cm.—(Stories of America)
    "Based on an interview that . . . John Waskowitz gave in 1974
to the Pittsburgh Oral History Project, sponsored by the
Pennsylvania Historical Museum and Commission"—Pref.
    Summary: Uses the experiences of an unemployed steel worker
and his family in Pittsburgh to describe the events of the economic depression that gripped the country from 1929 through 1933.
    ISBN 0-8114-7229-9 — ISBN 0-8114-8069-0 (softcover)
    1. Unemployed—Pennsylvania—Pittsburgh—Juvenile litera-
ture. 2. Iron and steel workers—Pennsylvania—Pittsburgh—
Juvenile literature. 3. Depressions—1929—Pennsylvania—
Pittsburgh—Juvenile literature. 4. Pittsburgh (Pa.)—Economic
conditions—Juvenile literature. [1. Depressions—1929.
2. Unemployed. 3. Pittsburgh (Pa.)—Economic conditions.]
I. Jones, Jan N., ill. II. Waskowitz, John, 1903-1982. III. Title.
IV. Series.
HD5726.P6N67   1993
330.9748'86042—dc20   92-18082
                                                   CIP
                                                   AC

ISBN 0-8114-7229-9 (Hardcover)
ISBN 0-8114-8069-0 (Softcover)

Introduction
by Alex Haley, General Editor

I was eight years old in 1929 when the Great Depression began. Hungry people, homeless people were everywhere. Times were hard. More people were out of work, out of money, and out of luck than at any time in our long history. People looked for help and there was none. Instead they were told to help themselves. Go on, pull yourself up by your bootstraps, they were told. But when they bent down to tug at their bootstraps, they discovered that the boots, straps and all, were gone. They had been worn away by the hard times.

We Want Jobs! is a story about the Great Depression. It is a story about how families and communities found new ways to get help for themselves. It is a story about caring, too. Looking around our towns and cities today you can see that we need to care a little more than we do. There are homeless people there. There are hungry people there. Again.

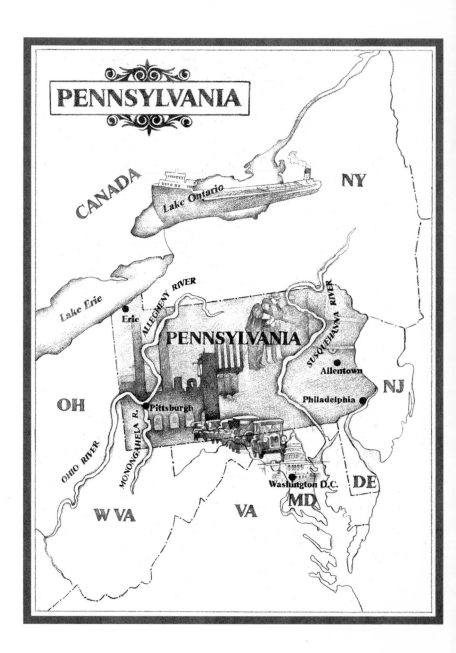

Contents

1

When the Work Stopped:
Port Vue, 1929

The sun burned away a morning fog and shone brightly on the green, two-story wooden house on Trimble Street. The sky was blue, the late fall air fresh and clean-smelling. Only the occasional train whistle broke the stillness outside.

Inside, Victoria Waskowitz dressed her two young children for church. It was a Sunday late in 1929. John Waskowitz came in from the vegetable garden behind the house. He held little John Junior, age one, while Victoria helped Jane, who was two, put on her dress. Then they put on their coats, and they all began the walk to church.

Trimble Street ran along a hill in the town of Port Vue, just outside Pittsburgh, Pennsylvania.

From the top of the hill, you could see two rivers meet—the big Monongahela and the smaller Youghiogheny. Beside the Monongahela, up and down the river, stood many big steel factories with giant smokestacks.

The Waskowitz family walked down the hill and crossed the smaller river. They went past a large building where beer was once made. The brewery had been closed for several years now. They also passed a meat-packing plant. It, too, was quiet.

When they got to Holy Family Church, they went inside and sat down to worship. On this Sunday, the church was full. There were more people than usual. But many of them, especially the men, looked sad. John Waskowitz, sitting with his family, didn't smile or exchange friendly greetings with his neighbors.

Why were they sad on this beautiful, sunny day? What was so wrong on this mild fall morning to make the young family so unhappy?

Normally the air in Port Vue was gray and sooty, as if a black snowstorm was raging. Most of the time the air carried a bitter, burning smell. The tall smokestacks of Pittsburgh and the surrounding factory towns usually coughed out end-

less clouds of thick, dark smoke. The steel mills normally roared and bellowed, sending huge streaks of flame leaping toward the sky. Even on a Sunday, the morning air should have been noisy and bright with fire. But it wasn't.

Most Sundays, women like Victoria Waskowitz struggled alone to get their young children ready for church. They made the short walk across the little river by themselves while their husbands and teenage sons went off to work in the factories.

In normal times, Victoria swept the coal soot off her front porch every day—otherwise it piled up like sand on a beach. Now she didn't have to. There was little soot in the air. Something was terribly wrong here.

Hard times had come in the form of an economic depression. Many people had lost their jobs. Factories and businesses were closing. Farmers were being thrown off their land, and their crops were rotting in the fields or in warehouses. People were going hungry.

In Port Vue and the other towns around Pittsburgh, the depression meant the steel factories weren't open every day. In fact, they were closed more often than they were open. Their smokestacks did not blow flame-red and soot-black clouds into the sky. The roar of busy factories no longer hushed the songs of birds or the whispers of the wind.

John and Victoria Waskowitz were worried. Without work they would run out of money. Without money they would be unable to pay their bills or buy new things.

Soon the stores where families like the Waskowitzes shopped were also suffering hard times. No one was buying their goods. No one had money. Stores began closing. More of the places where new things were made began to close. The depression was like a long line of toppling dominoes.

This depression became so bad that it was soon known as "The Great Depression," the worst in the history of the United States. Before long, one out of every four workers in America would be out of a job. They were healthy, strong, and eager for work, but the jobs were gone.

All during 1929, John Waskowitz had walked every morning to a steel factory down the hill and across the small river from his house. All during that awful year, he waited outside the factory gates to find out if there was work that day or not. Usually there was none.

John had been working on hard jobs in steel

plants since he was fourteen years old. He was a hard and able worker. He was good at his job. But now he was twenty-six and he could get work only one day a month. One day of work a month would not feed his family.

The fresh air, the clear skies, and the quiet stillness were proof of the economic depression in Pittsburgh, "the Steel City." Now, most of the city's 250,000 steel workers had lost their jobs. Something was very wrong here: no work.

2

What to Do?
Port Vue, 1931

John Waskowitz stood in a line outside the gates of a steel factory. It was 1931. The long line snaked around the factory. It wasn't a line of workers waiting to work. It was a line of hungry men waiting for food. John's company was giving out boxes of food to their unemployed workers. John waited in line for a box. So did many other men: workers, foremen, supervisors. All were waiting quietly for their food boxes.

The men wore their hats low on their brows. Their collars were turned up high against their cheeks. Their faces were turned away from the street toward the bars of the factory gates. They were ashamed to be in this line. They were ashamed that someone had to give them food. They were ashamed that they were out of work.

Things had gotten worse for John. Now he didn't even work once a month. He was completely unemployed. The Waskowitzes had emptied their bank account. John had turned in his insurance policy for money, but it had been spent, too. There was nowhere else for him to turn for money. As much as he hated charity,[1] as ashamed as he was for having to depend on someone to give him food, he had no other choice. How else would his family survive?

At the head of the line sat a man at a desk. He had a giant notebook with people's names in it. He checked each name off as the men came forward. More than a few were turned away by the man with the book. Some because they hadn't worked at the factory long enough. Some because they hadn't worked there at all. The factory gave these men nothing.

As they came before the man with the notebook, they showed their nervousness. They looked down at their worn shoes. They fidgeted.

---

[1] food, money, or other help given to the poor

Some stared past the man at the table to the closed factory behind him. Each man wondered if he would be turned away after all the waiting.

John's turn came. Slowly, the man wet his thumb and turned the pages of the notebook. He ran his finger slowly down the length of several pages, searching for John's name. John looked around. What was taking this guy so long? Finally, his name was found and checked. A square brown box was pushed toward him.

As soon as John got his box away from the table, he inspected its contents. In it was a bag of navy beans, a slab of bacon, a square of margarine, a five-pound sack of flour. He closed the box carefully and tucked it under his arm. He was ready for the walk home.

But when John looked up he saw a sight that stopped him dead in his tracks. All around him were streams of people carrying boxes under their arms. They looked identical. Tired-looking men in dark work clothes carrying brown boxes. They all looked so sad. All of them might as well have been carrying signs that said, "I'm out of work. I can't take care of my family. I'm a failure."

John retreated around a corner and sat down in the shadows until dark. In the dark no one would see him going home with his box.

No one likes to feel helpless. John felt helpless. More than anything he wanted a job. Until the Depression there had always been work to be found somewhere. If not in Port Vue, then in McKeesport or Braddock or Homestead. If not in any of these places, then in Pittsburgh or faraway McKees Rocks. Work had slowed before, but this was the first time it had stopped so completely. No one could remember a time when you could look day after day after day for a job and not find one.

Workers showed up by the hundreds when word got out about a job somewhere. Hundreds of workers all trying for the same job. Hundreds of workers turned away when the position was filled.

Once John heard a rumor of work at a factory far up the Monongahela. He was up and out of the house before the sun broke over the surrounding hills. He walked all morning to reach the factory ten miles away. On his way, he passed one big steel plant after another. Each one was closed. John kept walking.

When John reached the factory he learned the rumor was false. There was no work to be had there. He had walked all that way for nothing. Sadly, he began the long trek home. Along the way he stopped at other factory gates. He would ask if there was any work. Always the answer was no.

The walk home seemed longer. It was lonely. Night was falling fast. Beneath the darkening sky, John approached one of the area's many bridges. Ahead of him he saw a man sitting on the bridge's railing. The hills banking the river that ran below grew deeper into the shadows. John found himself walking faster. There was something alarming about the man on the railing.

John began to run toward the man, but he was too late. The man jumped from the railing. He fell in a strange silence. John heard nothing as he ran forward. His heart thumped with horror and shock as he reached the railing. Below he could barely see the man's still form in the shallow water. He lay not far from the river bank.

Frightened, John hurried along. Then, he saw another man—a man who already looked like a ghost—walk in front of a speeding train. The train hit the man and killed him. John wondered in horror: Did the man do this on purpose, or was he just lost in his worries? John's walk of hope had turned into a nightmare.

At home John told Victoria about the terrible things he had seen on his long walk. He whispered to her—so that the children couldn't hear—that some men wanted to die rather than live in such hopeless times. This isn't right, he told Victoria. *None* of it is right. There should be work for people who want it. There should be help that doesn't make people feel shame because there are no jobs for them. These ideas burned in John's heart. But what could he do about them?

3

Marching for Jobs:
Washington, D.C., 1932

The people of Port Vue tried to help one another make it through the Depression. The Waskowitzes and their neighbors shared food from their backyard gardens. Victoria baked bread. Extra loaves were traded for other food supplies. She sewed and patched worn clothes. Growing children were a problem to keep in clothes. Hand-me-downs helped. Neighbors exchanged clothes from child to child.

Fuel for cooking and heating was a problem. Near the Waskowitzes' house were some abandoned coal mines. Neighbors gathered there to scrape up sacks of free coal. Young people gathered coal for old people. The free coal helped people stay warm in the winter. It helped fuel ovens so people could cook meals and bake.

Because they had a warm house and food, the Waskowitzes were luckier than many. Many people lost their homes. Some people lived in their cars. Others lived in shacks made of cardboard or old wooden crates. Whole villages of shacks were built in parks and under bridges.

People began calling villages of the homeless "Hoovervilles." Herbert Hoover was President of the United States at the time. Many people blamed him for the Depression. And they blamed him for not doing enough to help people in trouble. Naming the villages "Hoovervilles" was their way of letting everyone know they thought it was President Hoover's fault that jobless people were living in cardboard boxes.

People living in Hoovervilles still needed food. Often they begged for food or money on the street. Sometimes they begged for bread or scraps at the kitchen doors of people who lived in real homes. Sometimes a church or community organization would set up a soup kitchen to feed the homeless.

In Pittsburgh, a priest named Father Cox started a big kitchen in the basement of his

church. Father Cox would beg bread from bakers, vegetables from grocers, and meat from butchers. Then he would serve the bread with the soup he made from the meat and vegetables. Homeless people would line up around the block for what might be their only meal of the day.

But Father Cox's kitchen didn't solve the problem of hunger any more than cardboard shacks solved the problem of homelessness. More was needed. People like Father Cox decided that if President Hoover didn't know what to do, well, they would tell him.

In 1932 Father Cox organized a trip to Washington, D.C. People who had no jobs were going to Washington to ask the President for help. Thousands of jobless workers from Pittsburgh and the nearby towns were going. John Waskowitz was one of them.

On a cold January morning a long parade of cars began the trip of several hundred miles from Father Cox's church to the White House. Each car was jammed full of unemployed workers. More people came than there was room for in the cars. So people walked, or hitched, or sneaked rides on freight trains. Altogether, Father Cox led 25,000 people to the nation's capital.

Months before, many of these men had stood with John on the food line outside the factory gates. Then they had been ashamed. They had felt defeated and helpless.

But now things were different. People no longer felt that it was their fault there were no jobs. And they no longer felt helpless. They were going to Washington to do something about it. Along the way, they were often cheered by people when they passed through towns or by farmhouses. When they stopped for gasoline, people gave them coffee and sandwiches.

When they got to Washington, John went with the group leaders to see their United States senator. We need work, they told the senator. They explained how a worker could look for a job for weeks and months and not find one. They told stories like the one John had whispered to Victoria the night he saw two men take their own lives in despair. Too many people still blamed themselves, they said. It was time for the government to do something.

The senator listened. Please help us, he was asked. We want jobs.

But the senator could not promise John and his friends jobs. Not by himself. Instead he gave them gas money for the trip back to Pittsburgh.

The unemployed workers did not give up. With Father Cox they visited the Secretary of the Treasury, who was from Pittsburgh. He, too, listened and gave a little of his own money to help. But he also said he couldn't help the men get jobs.

John and his friends continued to knock on the doors of anybody who might be able to help them. Some officials listened. Some called them troublemakers and refused to talk to them.

One senator offered to put John and a group of his friends in a movie newsreel. The senator was running for re-election that year. He thought American voters wanted the sale of beer to be made legal again. (Alcoholic drinks had been made illegal in the United States twelve years earlier.)

The senator wanted to make a speech for the newsreel cameras with John and his friends standing behind him. He wanted them to chant, "We want beer! We want beer!" This newsreel would be shown in movie theaters all over the country. It might make the senator very popular.

John and his friends agreed to stand behind the senator while they filmed the newsreel. The senator stood on the steps of the Capitol. He made his speech. Someone signalled the jobless workers to begin their chant. The men shouted out, "We want *jobs!* We want *jobs!*"

The startled senator spun around. He glared at the chanting men. The camera kept filming. "We want jobs! We want jobs!"

Father Cox tried to take this same message to President Hoover. The country had never gone through anything like this before. The government should do something, he felt, and the President should lead the way.

But the President refused to meet with Father Cox. Disappointed, the jobless parade began the long trip back to Pittsburgh. They were worried about the future but determined to get help. They wanted *jobs*.

4

A New Deal:
Port Vue, 1933

Victoria Waskowitz sat quietly by the coal stove in the green house on Trimble Street. It was a cold evening early in March 1933. A pot of beans bubbled on the stove. Jane, now almost six, and John Junior, who was four, were seated at the table. Dinner would be ready soon. It was warm in the kitchen by the stove.

A cold draft of air passed through and the gaslights winked on and off. Electricity had not yet come to the Waskowitzes' neighborhood. The gas lamps often flickered in the night wind.

Sometimes the wind would make a noise, and the children would look expectantly at the door. They were eager for their father to come home.

He had gone to Washington again, this time to take part in a celebration. The United States had a new President, one John and Victoria had helped elect.

But their father had been gone three days now, and Jane and John Junior kept asking when he would be home. Soon, their mother would answer, soon. He should be home soon. Maybe before supper was ready so he could eat with them, she thought to herself.

The three days John had been gone seemed like three months to the children. And "soon" seemed like forever. They didn't like it when their father was away. So the questions continued. They continued with each windknock and floorboard creak. Is that him? Will he be home soon? Victoria finally stopped answering. Instead she served them their supper.

Victoria was just as eager for John to come home as the children were. She was busy enough when he was home. With him gone, she had even more chores and responsibilities. But it was only three days, and this was something really special.

Victoria imagined John in the huge crowd in Washington. The hopeful speeches. The patriotic music. The pomp and ceremony. Yesterday she had heard all about it from neighbors across the river. Electricity had come to the other side of the river where the shops and church were. People there had heard the inauguration[2] on the radio.

One neighbor told how a whole group of people gathered in a friend's living room to listen to the inauguration. In the center of the room stood a radio fixed in a big cabinet of polished wood. Everyone piled close to it. The owner fiddled with its shiny knobs. First it whistled. Then it squeaked. Then there was a sound like the wind through summer leaves. Finally they could hear the broadcast clear as the hourly ringing of the nearby church bells.

The neighbor said everything had gone well. We have a new President, she reported to Victoria.

John must have been so thrilled to be there as the new President took the oath of office. Ever since he had returned from Washington with Father Cox and the 25,000 marchers, John had worked to elect a new President. Their trip had

---

[2] ceremony at which a President takes the oath of office

convinced them that President Hoover didn't care about their troubles. He didn't care about working people who had lost their jobs. Someone new was needed. Someone who did care.

At a big meeting in Port Vue, Father Cox had urged people to vote for change. John and Victoria were there and they had brought many of their neighbors, too. They joined Father Cox in trying to convince everyone that it was time for a change—time to support the man who was running against President Hoover.

This man's name was Franklin D. Roosevelt, and he promised to make things better if he could.

Roosevelt seemed to care more than President Hoover. While Hoover seemed content to wait the Depression out, Roosevelt seemed eager to do something about it. He said he would use the government to help people who had lost their jobs. He promised the people of the United States a "new deal." John and Victoria liked what they heard from Franklin Roosevelt. He made the kind of promises John and Father Cox and all the other jobless workers had tried to get President Hoover to make. Millions of other American voters also liked the idea of a new deal. They voted for

Roosevelt for President, and he won the election.

Voting that Tuesday in November had felt very good indeed to Victoria Waskowitz. And when she and John heard that Roosevelt had won—well, they felt as if they'd really done something. They had taken part in history.

Suddenly the front door opened with a bang. There was no mistaking that noise! Jane and John Junior were down in a flash from their chairs. Their father was home!

John caught the two running children in a hug and kissed Victoria hello over his clinging, giggling children. They were all happy to be together again.

John was hungry after his long trip back from Washington, but he was too excited to eat. There was too much to tell. He sat down, resting his elbows on the table, his dinner cooling as he spoke in a rush of new memories.

He told them thousands and thousands of people had gathered around the Capitol steps for the inauguration. People were packed together like sardines, but no one seemed to mind. Soldiers and police were everywhere.

Chatter ran through the crowd like ripples across a pond on a windy day. Most of the talk came from people who thought they had spotted Mr. Roosevelt. Look! Is that the new President coming? I think that's him off to the left. Can you see him? But some people were discussing more serious news. Did you hear that an assassin[3] tried to kill Roosevelt a few weeks ago in Miami? Is that why all the police are here? Many people in the crowd were worried. They finally had reason to hope, and they did not want anything to destroy that hope—not after they'd come this far. Sudden noises caused moments of fear. But there was no need for panic. Everything went fine. It was a glorious day.

When Mr. Roosevelt and President Hoover finally arrived, everyone stood tall, leaning this way and that to get a better view. It was really something to see. In just a few short minutes, the two men had changed roles. Franklin Roosevelt, hand on Bible, took the oath of office and became *President* Franklin Roosevelt. And at the same time, President Hoover became *Mister* Hoover.

Then the new President made a speech. With a voice that was crisp and precise, President

---

[3] killers who murder leaders

Roosevelt promised to "speak the truth, the whole truth, frankly and boldly." He said that the nation would endure and would prosper again.

"So first of all," he continued, "let me assert my firm belief that the only thing we have to fear is fear itself."

This was the first of many things that John had been eager to hear. It had been fear of the future that led that man to jump to his death—and he had not been alone in his fear. People needed to have courage, to have faith in the future. But it wasn't easy when the problems were so big. John knew that as well as anyone.

The President began to list the problems that faced the nation. One by one he addressed each issue: property values down, taxes up, trade down, savings gone, crops with no markets.

Then he said, "More important, a host of unemployed citizens face the grim problem of existence. And an equally great number toil with little return. Only a foolish optimist[4] can deny the dark realities of the moment."

The President wasn't sugar-coating the truth.

---

[4] person who always believes things are fine and getting better

"This nation," he went on to say, "asks for action, and action *now*. Our greatest primary task is to put people to work."

That, more than anything else, was what John Waskowitz wanted to hear. It was as if the President was answering the chant of John's earlier trip to Washington. "We want jobs! We want jobs!" It had been their battle cry. Now the President of the United States was saying we must put people to work.

John couldn't have been happier as he described all this to Victoria. The children listened and yawned. It was late now, and they were sleepy. They understood little of what John and Victoria talked about that night. But they did know that their parents were happy, and somehow they knew that this feeling would still be there tomorrow when they woke up.

Epilogue

A Better Life

President Roosevelt kept his word. He took action immediately, doing his best to end the Great Depression. The government tried to feed, clothe, and house those in great need. It tried to find jobs for the jobless. It put people to work planting trees, cleaning streets, building dams, bridges, and highways. Writers, artists, teachers, and performers were hired to write guidebooks and instructional manuals, decorate buildings, teach poor people, and entertain people everywhere.

Many of the things President Roosevelt tried didn't work. But people were glad that he took action; he tried new ideas and reworked old ones. It showed people that he cared and that he believed problems could be solved. If that doesn't work, try this. And if this doesn't do the trick, we'll try something else. That seemed to be his attitude and it gave courage to people like John and Victoria Waskowitz. It gave them confidence and hope.

The Great Depression didn't end with the President's speech. And it didn't end with all the activity of his first year in office. It kept on. But things got better. Slowly but surely, they got better.

For the Waskowitz family conditions improved earlier than most. On May 15, 1933, John's thirtieth birthday, he received a wonderful present. He got his job back! The steel factory reopened and John was needed at the plant. Soon he was working every day again. Voting had helped make a better life for John and his family.

After he went back to work, John tried to get Allegheny County—the county where he lived—to help poor people more. He wanted the county government to do more. In 1934, John worked with others who felt as he did to elect two new Allegheny County Commissioners. Their candidates won the election. The county now had leaders who wanted to help the many workers who remained without jobs.

John soon got a job in the county government. He gave up his job at the steel factory, and someone else took it. John worked for the county government until he retired in 1968. John died in 1982, and Victoria died four years later in 1986. Their children and grandchildren still live and work in the Pittsburgh area.

Afterword

This story was based on an interview given by a man named John Waskowitz in 1974 to the Pittsburgh Oral History Project. This project was sponsored by the Pennsylvania Historical Museum and Commission, which has kindly given its permission to use the interview as the basis for this book. The author of the story then did several additional interviews with Mr. Waskowitz's family.

The descriptive details in this story are all factual. The people in the story are all real people. A conversation or speech in quotes means it is an exact or almost exact quote. A conversation or speech that is not in quotes shows what might have been said, based on the information we have.

Notes

Page 5 The Great Depression did not occur overnight. Conditions had been building up to a depression for a long time. The 1920s were very prosperous, but not for farmers, who struggled through much of the decade. Nor were they prosperous for such people as coal miners and textile workers. These people labored under poor working conditions and received low wages for their efforts.

Additionally, many people who did benefit had a false prosperity. They were buying on credit, which made them vulnerable to changes in the economy. Thousands of people were borrowing money to buy stocks, which rocketed to new heights during the boom. Then, when the stock market crashed in October 1929, billions of dollars were lost. People could not pay for the items bought on credit. Businesses closed, causing workers to lose their jobs and their homes.

Pages 8–9 "They were ashamed. . . ." Even though the workers had done nothing wrong, they felt the Depression was their fault. They believed that something was wrong with them if they couldn't find work, and didn't have money to pay their bills and buy food.

Page 9 In 1931 there was no unemployment insurance, no social security, and no state or federal welfare programs. Unemployed workers were on their own. They had to look to charity for help. Many people couldn't bear to do this. They felt that accepting charity meant they couldn't take care of themselves. It made them feel helpless.

Page 15 Many people helped each other during the Great Depression. For example, a chef who worked at a restaurant in New York was allowed to take home leftover food. Not only did he use the food to feed his family, but he also was able to feed other children in the neighborhood.

Page 16 President Hoover received much of the blame for the Great Depression. He seemed not to care about the troubles Americans were having. He believed that the economy would straighten itself out in a few months without help from the government. However, when he realized that businesses would not be able to solve their own problems and help end the Depression, Hoover did act. He got Congress to pass laws enabling the government to provide help to businesses and individuals. One law set up the Reconstruction Finance Corporation, which loaned money to banks and other businesses to help keep them from closing. Another bill provided credit for homeowners and farmers. His support of public works and conservation programs helped provide jobs for some who were unemployed. Unfortunately for him politically, Hoover's actions were too little and too late. Franklin Roosevelt won election by promising to balance the budget, help the unemployed, aid farmers, and end Prohibition.

Page 18 Marches on Washington, D.C., have been a common way for Americans to express their opinion about something. For example, a group of unemployed World War I veterans marched on Washington in June 1932. They were demanding early payment of a bonus promised them for their military service during the war. President Hoover sent out troops to disperse the veterans. This act reinforced people's belief that Hoover was reluctant to take positive action to halt the impact of the Depression.

Page 33 In spite of his physical disability due to polio, Franklin D. Roosevelt left his mark on the American scene. He is the only President ever to serve more than two terms in succession. During his first administration, he appointed Frances Perkins Secretary of Labor, making her the first woman ever named to a Cabinet post. His presidency also saw the passage of the Social Security Act of 1935, which authorized unemployment relief and old-age pensions. He also introduced the National Labor Relations Act of 1935, which strengthened the right of workers to settle disputes with management through collective bargaining. Roosevelt was also President during World War II. His "Day of Infamy" speech, in which the United States declared war on Japan, signalled our entry into World War II.

Robert J. Norrell is the director of the Center for Southern History and Culture at the University of Alabama. He is also the author of a number of books, including the prize-winning *Reaping the Whirlwind: The Civil Rights Movement in Tuskegee.*